Jaaz Nspiration

Impacting Lives and Making a Difference

Jacqueline Marie Norris, M.A.Ed

Jaaz Nspiration

Impacting Lives and Making a Difference

Jacqueline Marie Norris, M.A.Ed

Published by:
Jaaz Creative Designs

Jaaz Creative Designs
PO BOX 347217
San Francisco, CA 94134
jaazworld@gmail.com

Cover Design: Jacqueline Marie Norris
Logo: Scott Tyler
Editor: Jia Arrieta

Book Concept Inspired by:
Donna Chestang "Diva" Jackson

Jaaz Nspiration Supporters:
Fatt Sak Records
Nicole Marie Haute Events
Suave Entertainment
Anytime Anywhere Notary Express
P3 (Prayer + Perseverance + Patience)
Evergreen Baptist Church, SF

Written and Printed within the United States of America

ISBN-13: 978-0-9998703-1-0
ISNB-10: 0999870319

JN Content

Jaaz Nspiration Purpose

Many years ago, I started a postcard ministry entitled, Balancing Everyday Life (B.E.L.). Subscribers would receive an inspirational postcard via United States Postal Service once a week to encourage them and help them get through the week. Well, as postage rates increased B.E.L mailings were reduced to twice a month, once a month, every two months, and eventually the B.E.L ministry was silent. In 2016, The Lord revealed a disturbing vision of chaos and devastation shadowing my life, my community, and the world. No matter where you were located you could see communities being torn apart, lack of spiritual foundations/interest, unjustifiable killings, the inflated housing market, rapid foreclosures, financial struggles, elderly abuse, child abduction, and many other countless acts of disrespect, devastation, and civil demise. In June 2016, with the intent to change the dynamics within my control, I began sending random text messages to a select group of people. As the months went on and interest was renewed the list expanded as did the inspirational messages.

On October 3, 2016 I formally launched Jaaz Nspiration (JN), a website that offers positive and sharable affirmations. The established goal of the ministry was to consistently reach out to others via the advancements of technology, to share and exchange messages of hope and reminders of love as given to me by God.

In 2017 I was blessed with a vision to take the ministry to another level, thus the development of this book. Keeping the same foundation and commitment, I am still excited when I imagine the impact it could have if more people vowed to express love to one another daily. In a collective effort, we would have the power to change our situations in addition to strengthening the lives and faith of others by simply exchanging encouraging words, lending an ear, giving our time, or offering a heartfelt hug when needed.

As you interact with the pages of the book, I pray that you will be inspired to stand with me as I continue to share God's word, impact lives, and make a difference.

Sharing 

Sharing your experiences with others has the potential to broaden someone's perspective, motivate them to set personal goals, and inspire a new or rejuvenated mindset. Invest in others and over time, change will manifest in your life and the lives of those you have shared with.

May your testimony uplift someone's spirit and give them a reason to dedicate their life to Christ.

Scripture

1 Thessalonians 5:11 (MSG)

So speak encouraging words to one another. Build up hope so you'll all be together in this, no one left out, no one left behind. I know you're already doing this; just keep on doing it.

Friends

Who is in your Circle? It is a good idea to periodically check your space to ensure that the people you are interacting with are producing good energy, promoting positivity, and supporting life balance. There is a time and season for everything. If your friendships are choking your growth, it is time to Exit!

May you seek and obtain healthy friendships that inspire you to be better, live better, and do better.

Scripture

Proverbs 27:9 (MSG)
Just as lotions and fragrance give sensual delight, a sweet friendship refreshes the soul.

Relationship

With so many negative things taking place and going on, take a moment to be thankful for the relationship you have with the Master, the blessings He bestowed upon you, the breath He gives you, the places He sent you, the troubles you have had, the accomplishments He has overseen, the devastation He spared you from, and most of all, for the bond that He is creating between you and those you interact with.

May the Lord continue to guide you in the direction for which He has prepared for you and your family.

If by chance you do not have a relationship with the Lord, today is a good day to make His acquaintance!

Scripture

Romans 5:1-2 (MSG)

By entering through faith into what God has always wanted to do for us—set us right with him, make us fit for him—we have it all together with God because of our Master Jesus. And that's not all: We throw open our doors to God and discover at the same moment that he has already thrown open his door to us. We find ourselves standing where we always hoped we might stand—out in the wide open spaces of God's grace and glory, standing tall and shouting our praise.

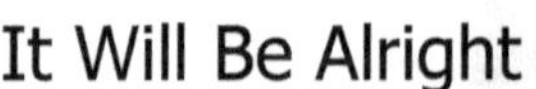

It Will Be Alright

God has everything under control, but you must have trust, be willing to shift thinking, be patient, and be willing to sacrifice. Emotions will eventually heal, relationships will be renewed, and finances will improve. Stand on God's word and watch as what seems difficult today transforms into freedom, life, and restoration over time.

May you be open to receive the countless blessings that God has in store for you today and in the days to come.

Scripture

1 Thessalonians 5:18 (MSG)

Be cheerful no matter what; pray all the time; thank God no matter what happens. This is the way God wants you who belong to Christ Jesus to live.

Yesterday

Today is a new day, rejoice! Leave yesterday where it is and be in love with the newness of this day.

May you find joy in the newness of today. May the worries, challenges, and sorrows of yesterday be a reminder of the need to rely on the Lord to provide a fresh start each day.

Scripture

Psalm 19:11-14 (MSG)

There's more: God's Word warns us of danger and directs us to hidden treasure. Otherwise how will we find our way? Or know when we play the fool? Clean the slate, God, so we can start the day fresh! Keep me from stupid sins, from thinking I can take over your work; Then I can start this day sun-washed, scrubbed clean of the grime of sin. These are the words in my mouth; these are what I chew on and pray. Accept them when I place them on the morning altar, O God, my Altar-Rock, God, Priest-of-My-Altar.

Worship

Your blessing and comfort begins with worship and is subject to what you believe and mostly who you believe in! Allow the Lord to guide you to your purpose. Do your best not to drive yourself to chaos, confusion, and sin.

May you be forever reminded of the LOVE that the Lord has for you. If you find yourself off track, spend time in prayer with the Lord and know that He has the POWER to renew, revive, and restore.

Scripture

Proverbs 3:5-12 (MSG)

Trust God from the bottom of your heart; don't try to figure out everything on your own. Listen for God's voice in everything you do, everywhere you go; he's the one who will keep you on track. Don't assume that you know it all. Run to God! Run from evil! Your body will glow with health, your very bones will vibrate with life! Honor God with everything you own; give him the first and the best. Your barns will burst, your wine vats will brim over. But don't, dear friend, resent God's discipline; don't sulk under his loving correction. It's the child he loves that God corrects; a father's delight is behind all this.

Confidence

You can do anything within Jesus Christ. Be confident, be open to change, and believe in yourself. Stand strong on your conviction and do not be tempted by the devil, he wants to ensure that you are defeated and weak.

May you realize your strength, gift, and talent then be able to use them to magnify and exalt the Lord.

Scripture

Galatians 5:22-23 (MSG)

But what happens when we live God's way? He brings gifts into our lives, much the same way that fruit appears in an orchard—things like affection for others, exuberance about life, serenity. We develop a willingness to stick with things, a sense of compassion in the heart, and a conviction that a basic holiness permeates things and people. We find ourselves involved in loyal commitments, not needing to force our way in life, able to marshal and direct our energies wisely.

Assurance

Let the newness of the day bring you assurance that while life can be challenging; in Jesus there is promise of a better tomorrow. Live, laugh, and exchange love on a daily basis.

May you forever be assured that in Jesus Christ the sun will always shine and offer blessings of love, hope, and forgiveness.

<u>Scripture</u>

Luke 1:78-79 (MSG)

Through the heartfelt mercies of our God, God's Sunrise will break in upon us, Shining on those in the darkness, those sitting in the shadow of death, Then showing us the way, one foot at a time, down the path of peace.

Community

Mr. Rogers is known for this statement: "It's a beautiful day in the neighborhood." As you look around your neighborhood, community, or environment ask yourself this question, "What can I do to beautify my surroundings?" You could sweep the streets, plant trees, and feed the homeless. You could extend God's love by volunteering your time, assisting the elderly, speaking out on injustice, refraining from the entertainment of gossip, reporting acts of violence, promoting positivity, praying for change, and by sharing the Word.

Opportunities are within your reach. Your voice and actions can lead to change. Do not be afraid to commit to your community!

May you find the motivation to impact the lives of those around you and make a difference in your community by displaying behaviors, attitudes, and using words that may encourage someone to turn to Christ or renew their faith in Him.

Scripture

Hebrews 6:9-12(MSG)

I have better things in mind for you—salvation things! God doesn't miss anything. He knows perfectly well all the love you've shown him by helping needy Christians,

Community

Continued

and that you keep at it. And now I want each of you to extend that same intensity toward a full-bodied hope, and keep at it till the finish. Don't drag your feet. Be like those who stay the course with committed faith and then get everything promised to them.

Truth 

The earth and its contents were not discovered - they were created.

Seek, Know, Acknowledge, Live, and Share the TRUTH.

May you embrace the TRUTH even when it contradicts what can be seen by the natural eye. Jesus is the Truth, the way, and the light!

<u>Scripture</u>

Genesis 1:1-2 (MSG)

First this: God created the Heavens and Earth—all you see, all you don't see. Earth was a soup of nothingness, a bottomless emptiness, an inky blackness. God's Spirit brooded like a bird above the watery abyss.

Reflection

Always make time to reflect on you, your actions, and your reactions. Duplicate the positives and refrain from repeating the negatives. Extend love and compassion; always celebrate the fact that you have the ability to live and enjoy life today!

May the reflection you see be one that encourages life and produces positive relationships today and in the future.

<u>Scripture</u>

1 Corinthians 16:13-14 (MSG)

Keep your eyes open, hold tight to your convictions, give it all you've got, be resolute, and love without stopping.

No More Excuses 

If you really want a blessing from the Lord, make HIM your priority, disclose your wants, desires, and/or limitations and as the days meet one to the next you will find yourself walking in and submerged in the newness of Life. Do not get distracted from the WAY, the TRUTH, or the LIFE. Let today be the day that you choose to eliminate excuses!

May you find a reason to remove excuses and limitations from your life so that you can live the life that God has prepared for you.

Scripture

1 John 1:6-7 (MSG)

If we claim that we experience a shared life with him and continue to stumble around in the dark, we're obviously lying through our teeth—we're not living what we claim. But if we walk in the light, God himself being the light, we also experience a shared life with one another, as the sacrificed blood of Jesus, God's Son, purges all our sin.

Love Overcomes Darkness 

God grants new mercy each morning. Who will you extend mercy and forgiveness to today? The love that runs through you has the ability to overcome hurt feelings, pain, wrong doing, and even guilt. Ask and seek forgiveness today and lift any burdens or dark shadows that have been lurking around the events of your life. Restored relationships and freedom start with forgiveness and are based on love!

May you be willing to forgive yourself and others so that goodness and mercy constantly finds its ways to those who you love and care about.

Scripture

Matthew 6:14-15 (MSG)

In prayer there is a connection between what God does and what you do. You can't get forgiveness from God, for instance, without also forgiving others. If you refuse to do your part, you cut yourself off from God's part.

Perspective

Today is a new day. What will you do different? A fresh attitude or perspective has the power to change behavior patterns and renew opinions about the past. Be well, live well, and love always!

May your perspective and attitude about life be a reflection of the love that Jesus has for you.

Scripture

1 Corinthians 13:1-7 (MSG)

If I speak with human eloquence and angelic ecstasy but don't love, I'm nothing but the creaking of a rusty gate. If I speak God's Word with power, revealing all his mysteries and making everything plain as day, and if I have faith that says to a mountain, "Jump," and it jumps, but I don't love, I'm nothing. If I give everything I own to the poor and even go to the stake to be burned as a martyr, but I don't love, I've gotten nowhere. So, no matter what I say, what I believe, and what I do, I'm bankrupt without love. Love never gives up. Love cares more for others than for self. Love doesn't want what it doesn't have. Love doesn't strut, Doesn't have a swelled head, Doesn't force itself on others, Isn't always "me first," Doesn't fly off the handle, Doesn't keep score of the sins of others, Doesn't revel when others grovel, Takes pleasure in the flowering of truth, Puts up with anything, Trusts God always, Always looks for the best,

Perspective

Continued

Never looks back, But keeps going to the end.

Influence and Power 

Influence and Power, social media has both. Be aware that the children and youth of today are more exposed and more sensitive than we were in our youth. Talk to them often and allow them the privilege of objective listening. You don't have to be their parent to save their life, change their mindset, heal their broken heart or direct them to the love of Christ.

May you find the courage, an understanding heart, and patience to listen, hear, and help the youth without judgment or criticism. Share the love of Jesus with them and encourage them to go to Him for comfort, wisdom, and understanding.

Scripture

Psalm 49:3-4 (MSG)

I set plainspoken wisdom before you, my heart-seasoned understandings of life. I fine-tuned my ear to the sayings of the wise, I solve life's riddle with the help of a harp.

Opportunity

Today is full of opportunities. What will you do today for society, your environment, your family, your friends, or yourself? Worrying about tomorrow will cause you more stress and anxiety than necessary. Take care of the business of today. Do your best not to put off things for tomorrow, as you will find that tomorrow will have its own challenges; thus, the things that are important may not receive your full attention. Prioritize your tasks accordingly.

May you seize the day and do the work that is required of you with a good attitude and positive mindset. May you find the strength to resist the stress, temptation, and anxiety of tomorrow.

Scripture

Ephesians 5:1-2 (MSG)

If you preach, just preach God's Message, nothing else; if you help, just help, don't take over; if you teach, stick to your teaching; if you give encouraging guidance, be careful that you don't get bossy; if you're put in charge, don't manipulate; if you're called to give aid to people in distress, keep your eyes open and be quick to respond; if you work with the disadvantaged, don't let yourself get irritated with them or depressed by them. Keep a smile on your face.

Be Mindful of Others 

While many are celebrating joyous events like birthdays, marriages, child birth, graduations, and life in general there are many who are experiencing or re-living heart ache, loss, guilt or dealing with some type of pain or emotional imbalance. The best news is that if they connect to the source they can reform their situation and receive healing. The death, burial and resurrection of Jesus Christ is the reason why joy can be found.

When you think of the blessings bestowed upon you as a result of the blood of Jesus, may it empower you to help others not to feel alone, depressed, or isolated this year. Being mindful of others is a gift that can be freely given every day.

Scripture

Ephesians 5:1-2 (MSG)

Watch what God does, and then you do it, like children who learn proper behavior from their parents. Mostly what God does is love you. Keep company with him and learn a life of love. Observe how Christ loved us. His love was not cautious but extravagant. He didn't love in order to get something from us but to give everything of himself to us. Love like that.

Monthly Review 

Take time today to review the events of the month, the challenges, the difficulties, the highs and lows, the achievements, the disappointments, the people that left, the people you met, the places you have been, the places you did not go etc. You may find that you have many reasons to be thankful for each experience, as each one has provided you with an opportunity to rejoice and proclaim victory. In most cases you have been blessed far beyond measure.

May you find it in your heart to rejoice and worship the Lord in and out of season, for all things work out in your favor!

Scripture

Psalm 138:1-3 (MSG)

Thank you! Everything in me says "Thank you!" Angels listen as I sing my thanks. I kneel in worship facing your holy temple and say it again: "Thank you!" Thank you for your love, thank you for your faithfulness; Most holy is your name, most holy is your Word. The moment I called out, you stepped in; you made my life large with strength.

Time Matters 

Be thankful for the opportunity to see another day. Today, do something that is worthy of doing, something that displays your natural instinct to love. Do something that will be memorable not just to you, but to the people in your circle. Embrace the opportunities of the day and make each moment count because tomorrow is not promised.

May the opportunities of today lead you to a better understanding of your purpose here on earth while giving someone around you a reason to smile.

Scripture

Matthew 10:40-42 (MSG)

"We are intimately linked in this harvest work. Anyone who accepts what you do, accepts me, the One who sent you. Anyone who accepts what I do accepts my Father, who sent me. Accepting a messenger of God is as good as being God's messenger. Accepting someone's help is as good as giving someone help. This is a large work I've called you into, but don't be overwhelmed by it. It's best to start small. Give a cool cup of water to someone who is thirsty, for instance. The smallest act of giving or receiving makes you a true apprentice. You won't lose out on a thing."

A Heavenly Friend 

Offering moral or spiritual support is much better than offering your opinion or judgment. Who really has your back and whose back do you really have? Being a "real" friend requires sacrifice, extending of love, a display of honesty, being truthful, and always being open to extend, receive, and accept forgiveness. Physical friends are necessary, but a Heavenly friend is a requirement for eternal life. When real friends let you down, God will always be there for you.

May you be true to yourself and optimistic with regards to your friend selection.

Scripture

Job 11:13-20 (MSG)

"Still, if you set your heart on God and reach out to him, If you scrub your hands of sin and refuse to entertain evil in your home, You'll be able to face the world unashamed and keep a firm grip on life, guiltless and fearless. You'll forget your troubles; they'll be like old, faded photographs. Your world will be washed in sunshine, every shadow dispersed by dayspring. Full of hope, you'll relax, confident again; you'll look around, sit back, and take it easy. Expensive, without a care in the world, you'll be hunted out by many for your blessing. But the wicked will see none of this. They're headed

A Heavenly Friend 

Continued

down a dead-end road with nothing to look forward to—nothing."

Continual Thanksgiving

Continue to express and celebrate the spirit of Thanksgiving throughout the year. You may not be where you want to be, but you are not where you used to be. That is enough of a reason to thank God daily. Continue to spread love, help your fellow man, and reach out to others. A kind word can save a life, fix a situation, increase joy or heal a broken heart.

May you display an attitude of thankfulness every morning when you rise. Ma y you sha e the gift of gratitude with someone experiencing pain, sadness or suffering from an unseen issue like a broken heart, mental imbalance, or a disease.

<u>Scripture</u>

Colossians 3:15-17 (MSG)

Let the peace of Christ keep you in tune with each other, in step with each other. None of this going off and doing your own thing. And cultivate thankfulness. Let the Word of Christ—the Message—have the run of the house. Give it plenty of room in your lives. Instruct and direct one another using good common sense. And sing, sing your hearts out to God! Let every detail in your lives—words, actions, whatever—be done in the name of the Master, Jesus, thanking God the Father every step of the way.

This is the Day 

This is the day that the Lord has made. Let us rejoice and be glad. Today if you have burdens, feel weighed down, overwhelmed by situations or not sure where to turn, look to the Lord for he can lift your burdens, free your spirit, and guide you to peace.

Rejoice, for today is a new day. Your glass is not half empty – it is half full.

May you change your perspective so that you can clearly see the blessings over your life and you can fully appreciate everything that you have, everything that you have been through, and every challenge that you have overcome.

Scripture

Psalm 146:1-9 (MSG)

Hallelujah! O my soul, praise God! All my life long I'll praise God, singing songs to my God as long as I live. Don't put your life in the hands of experts who know nothing of life, of salvation life. Mere humans don't have what it takes; when they die, their projects die with them. Instead, get help from the God of Jacob, put your hope in God and know real blessing! God made sky and soil, sea and all the fish in it. He always does what he says—he defends the wronged, he feeds the hungry.

This is the Day 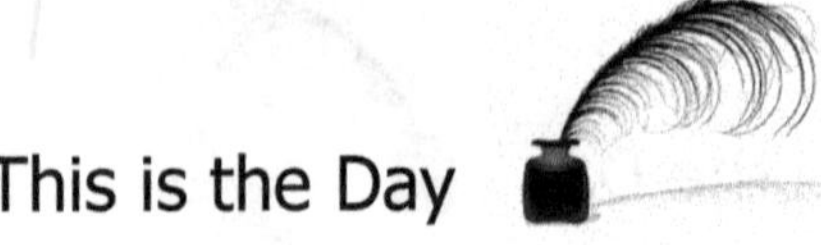

Continued

God frees prisoners— he gives sight to the blind, he lifts up the fallen. God loves good people, protects strangers, takes the side of orphans and widows, but makes short work of the wicked.

Own Your Blessing 

You have the power to create balance in your life by exercising a positive attitude, good behavior, and healthy thoughts. Do not let the craziness of the day or the craziness of others dictate your mood or alter your thinking. Today, own your blessings and put yourself in a position to receive the goodness you deserve and desire.

May you freely step into your blessings and walk into the newness of life under the guidance of the Holy Spirit.

<u>Scripture</u>

Deuteronomy 28:1-6 (MSG)

If you listen obediently to the Voice of God, your God, and heartily obey all his commandments that I command you today, God, your God, will place you on high, high above all the nations of the world. All these blessings will come down on you and spread out beyond you because you have responded to the Voice of God, your God: God's blessing inside the city, God's blessing in the country; God's blessing on your children, the crops of your land, the young of your livestock, the calves of your herds, the lambs of your flocks. God's blessing on your basket and bread bowl; God's blessing in your coming in, God's blessing in your going out.

Success

The keys to spiritual success equates to Christ like character, behavior, and attitude, NOT money and status. Money and status are temporary! Display traits of honesty & compassion. If you are seeking real success, demonstrate behavior that is acceptable unto the Lord, and an attitude that reflects positivity and grace.

May you realize that your spiritual success is a reflection of your foundation in Christ. Your ability to share that success with others may help introduce someone to the kingdom of heaven and allow them to claim their long-awaited blessing.

Scripture

1 Samuel 2:6-10 (MSG)

God brings death and God brings life, brings down to the grave and raises up. God brings poverty and God brings wealth; he lowers, he also lifts up. He puts poor people on their feet again; he rekindles burned-out lives with fresh hope, Restoring dignity and respect to their lives—a place in the sun! For the very structures of earth are God's; he has laid out his operations on a firm foundation. He protectively cares for his faithful friends, step by step, but leaves the wicked to stumble in the dark.

Success 

Continued

No one makes it in this life by sheer muscle! God's enemies will be blasted out of the sky, crashed in a heap and burned. God will set things right all over the earth, he'll give strength to his king, he'll set his anointed on top of the world!

Achievement

You can achieve what seems to be impossible when you put your trust in the Lord and allow Him to be the one who orders your steps. Welcome the opportunity to learn something new on a regular basis and embrace the challenges that are presented. In many instances those challenges will be your inspiration. You need to remain focused on achievement and future success!

May your eyes be opened to your true blessings. May your future be filled with feelings of satisfaction and achievement at all times.

<u>Scripture</u>

2 Thessalonians 1:11-12 (MSG)

Because we know that this extraordinary day is just ahead, we pray for you all the time—pray that our God will make you fit for what he's called you to be, pray that he'll fill your good ideas and acts of faith with his own energy so that it all amounts to something. If your life honors the name of Jesus, he will honor you. Grace is behind and through all of this, our God giving himself freely, the Master, Jesus Christ, giving himself freely.

A Glimpse of Happiness

Praying that today will be productive, filled with respectful exchanges, and present the opportunity to bring a smile to someone's face. Be open to doing something out of the ordinary for others (known or unknown) simply for the joy of filling them with a glimpse of happiness or real love. Exchanges of love tend to bring blessings to you, your household, and your environment.

May you be a blessing to someone; offer them the opportunity to feel loved, cared for, and relevant.

Scripture

Philippians 2:1-4 (MSG)

If you've gotten anything at all out of following Christ, if his love has made any difference in your life, if being in a community of the Spirit means anything to you, if you have a heart, if you care— then do me a favor: Agree with each other, love each other, be deep-spirited friends. Don't push your way to the front; don't sweet-talk your way to the top. Put yourself aside, and help others get ahead. Don't be obsessed with getting your own advantage. Forget yourselves long enough to lend a helping hand.

Basic Definition of Prayer

Prayer is simply a way to communicate with God the Father, the Son, and the Holy Spirit. There will be times in your life where you will have the urge/need to communicate with the one who can truly make a difference in your life. The following four prayers can be prayed as often as necessary and can be used as a supplement to your personal individual prayers or to help you get into the routine of having open dialogue with the Master.

In 1 Thessalonians 5:17 Paul reminds us to "pray without ceasing" and in Ephesians 6:18a we are told "And pray in the Spirit on all occasions with all kinds of prayers and requests".

Prayer changes things!

Notes/Reflection:

Prayer for Guidance

Lord watch over and protect me as well as everyone within my reach from hurt, harm, and danger.

Lord, please guide my foot steps and create opportunities for us to live according to your will.

Lord, help us to be a light to the dark stricken world and to be an example for those seeking a place in your kingdom.

Please Lord present your guidance as I seek an abundance of laughter, love, strength, and impactful interactions today and the days to come.

In Jesus name I present my request,

Amen!

Daily Prayer

Lord, today I am petitioning you, I am asking that my prayers and needs be met according to your will. When I am feeling depleted or lacking strength please Lord immediately energize and fill me with the Love and Comfort of the Holy Spirit.

Lord when all is well, and I feel positive and full of energy please present the opportunity for me to find the time to share those feelings and lift the spirit of someone in need.

Lord, grant patience as I interact with people and direct me to someone who needs to smile and feel loved today!

Lord, I thank you for everything that you have done and will do for me and my family. Thank you for each member in my family, I ask that you forgive us for our sins, cover us, keep us together, and remind us to forever be open to receiving your word.

I thank you for the opportunity to be an example of love, hope, and life.

In Jesus name I pray,

Amen!

Prayer for Comfort

Lord, fill me with the comfort of knowing that you are real and that you have the ability to fix my situation and protect me from the temptation of doing things that generate a negative impact on me and others.

God, I know that you are able and will continue to wave your hand of mercy over my life, my situations, and my family.

Thank you for continuously caring for me, loving me, forgiving me, making a way for me, and blessing me even when I do not deserve it.

In Jesus name I pray,

Amen!

Jaaz Prayer for your Strength

Dear Heavenly Father, May the person reading these words be filled with impeccable strength. May they be able to endure all of the challenges and obstacles that appear to be stubbing blocks to their faith and/or growth.

Lord, I ask that they be physically inspired and spiritually strengthened. Please Lord, equip them with the tools and resources they need to witness for you while respecting the diversity that you created.

Lord, I thank you for the opportunity to impact and to make a difference in their life. Lord, I ask that something within the pages of this book ignite a fire within that cannot be put out. I pray that they continue to seek you for wisdom, love, strength, comfort, and most of all eternal life. May they realize and be forever reminded that immediate restoration and healing comes from you.

In closing, may the strength they need from day to day be found in the creases of their faith.

In the name of our Lord and Savior Jesus Christ, I pray.

Amen!

Resource Scriptures

When all else fails, turn to the Word for inspiration, strength, motivation, love, peace, hope, and connection with the Holy Spirit.

1 Thessalonians 5:16-18 (NIV) Rejoice always, pray continually, give thanks in all circumstances; for this is God's will for you in Christ Jesus.

Philippians 4:6-7 (NIV) Do not be anxious about anything, but in every situation, by prayer and petition, with thanksgiving, present your requests to God. And the peace of God, which transcends all understanding, will guard your hearts and your minds in Christ Jesus.

1 John 5:14 (NIV) This is the confidence we have in approaching God: that if we ask anything according to his will, he hears us.

Psalm 145:18 (NIV) The Lord is near to all who call on him, to all who call on him in truth.

Acknowledgement

Thank you Lord for the vision! Thank you for the opportunity to reach the world, to impact lives and to make a difference with sincere words, a bright smile, and a comforting warm hug.

Thank you to everyone who supported me during this journey. Thank you for your words of encouragement, your love, your time, your energy, your ears, and most of all your trust. I appreciate you and without each of you I could not have accomplished all that I have thus far in my life.

To my children, Richard, Reinard, Reese, Reinika, and Rikki I love each of you for your individuality and your free-spirited way of living/thinking while it often contradicts with my way of thinking, I appreciate what I have learned from each of you.

Reese and Rikki, from conception to this very day you have been my motivation. I pray that the life that I live before your eyes is one that demonstrates that nothing is impossible, love is enviable, forgiveness can be granted, trust is critical, taking risks can lead to freedom, life should be shared not stored, and that God is real.

Acknowledgement 

Continued

To my husband, Richard Leonard Norris, Jr., thank you for everything you do, which is everything I stopped doing so that I could pursue my personal, educational, and spiritual goals. Thank you for showing me that it is ok to be me regardless of what people think or say. Thank you for continually encouraging me to draw my own picture instead of trying to paint myself into someone else's scene. Thank you for supporting me as I out grew the pre-assembled box that I was "assigned".

To my partner, Leesha Nicole Langlois, without you I could not have made it through the tough times, the decision-making process, and the times when defeat was knocking at my door. Thank you for staying up with me 'til the crack of dawn and for watching me sleep when I should have been working.

To my parents, thank you for the union that brought me into this world. I thank the Lord for using you as a vessel to usher me into existence.

Jaaz Closing Thought 

If everyone perceived themselves as lifelong learners, introducing new or different perspectives would have a dramatic impact on our society, family structure, and individual self-esteem. Being open to engage in a respectful approach toward conflict resolution and building strong foundations within individual communities promotes change as well as encourages people to love one another and exchange positive energy.

As an adult educator, I firmly believe that offering creative and inspiring words of encouragement has the potential to effectively bring change to a dying world. The right message at the right time can repair peer relationships, bring awareness, change minds, establish a loving (peaceful) environment, introduce love, resolve conflict, improve emotional situations, and inspire others to press on.

Improving our daily lives can be as simple as putting action to the following words: Create, Find, Maintain, Impact, and Balance.

No matter where you live, your ethnic background, gender, sexual orientation, marital status, education level, political status, pay grade, etc., "You have the power to make a difference".

I pray that you have been blessed by the words within and will share this experience with others.

Visit Jaazworld.wixsite.com/inspire or scan the box below for more Jaaz Nspiration.

Visit Jaazworld.wixsite.com/norris or scan the box below to view the Jacque Norris, Handcrafted Collection featuring greeting cards, papercrafts, and jewelry.

Upcoming Publications

Jaaz Nspiration Childrens Prayer Book

Jaaz Nspiration Volume 2

Jaaz Nspiraional Journey

Reflection/Notes

Reflection/Notes

www.ingramcontent.com/pod-product-compliance
Lightning Source LLC
Chambersburg PA
CBHW060202070426
42447CB00033B/2309

* 9 7 8 0 9 9 9 8 7 0 3 1 0 *